A Donation has been made to the
Clay County Public Library In
Memory Of:

Lillian White

This Donation has been made by:

Stephen & Melana Chitwood

THOMAS ALVA EDISON

INVENTOR AND ENTREPRENEUR

Clay County Public
Library
116 Guffey Street
Celina, TN 38551
(931) 243-3442

GREG ROZA

Britannica
Educational Publishing

IN ASSOCIATION WITH

ROSEN
EDUCATIONAL SERVICES

Published in 2015 by Britannica Educational Publishing (a trademark of Encyclopædia Britannica, Inc.) in association with The Rosen Publishing Group, Inc.
29 East 21st Street, New York, NY 10010

Distributed exclusively by Rosen Publishing.
To see additional Britannica Educational Publishing titles, go to rosenpublishing.com.

First Edition

Britannica Educational Publishing
J. E. Luebering: Director, Core Reference Group
Mary Rose McCudden: Editor, Britannica Student Encyclopedia

Rosen Publishing
Hope Lourie Killcoyne: Executive Editor
Heather Moore Niver: Editor
Nelson Sá: Art Director
Nicole Russo: Designer
Cindy Reiman: Photography Manager

Library of Congress Cataloging-in-Publication Data

Roza, Greg.
Thomas Alva Edison / Greg Roza. — First edition.
    pages cm.—(Britannica beginner bios)
Includes bibliographical references and index.
ISBN 978-1-62275-693-3 (library bound) — ISBN 978-1-62275-694-0 (pbk.) —
ISBN 978-1-62275-695-7 (6-pack)
1. Edison, Thomas A. (Thomas Alva), 1847–1931—Juvenile literature. 2. Inventors—United States—Biography—Juvenile literature. I. Title.
TK140.E3R76 2014
621.3092—dc23
[B]
                                                                                              2014018410

Manufactured in the United States of America

CONTENTS

CHAPTER ONE

THE WIZARD OF MENLO PARK

In this photograph from around 1877, Thomas Edison poses with his tinfoil phonograph.

From an early age, Thomas Edison loved to experiment and to learn how things work. As he grew up, he developed his own ways of thinking and working. After he opened a

Quick Fact

In 1862 Edison saved a young boy from being hit by a train. The boy's father worked for the railroad. He taught Edison how to use the telegraph and found a job for him.

Edison stops work to pose for a photograph in his workshop in 1906.

The phonograph is one of Edison's best-known inventions.

large workshop in Menlo Park, New Jersey, Edison shocked the world with all of his inventions.

Edison was always working on something new. He also improved on the designs of machines that already existed. Edison made them easier for regular people to buy and take care of. He soon earned the nickname the "Wizard of Menlo Park."

Edison invented some very useful products. In fact, we still use a lot of them today, like lightbulbs. Edison also made money selling everything people needed to use his products.

Thomas Edison left a lasting LEGACY. He is honored for his inventions. Most people agree that our world would not be the same without him.

Vocabulary Box

A LEGACY is something passed from one person to future people.

CHAPTER TWO

EARLY LIFE

Thomas Alva Edison was born on February 11, 1847, in Milan, Ohio. When he was about seven, the family moved to Port Huron, Michigan. Edison showed an early interest in experimenting with machines and chemicals. He did not do very well in school, so his mother helped him at home. She guided his interest in reading and learning.

As a boy, Edison sold candy and newspapers on the Grand Trunk Railroad, which ran between Port Huron and Detroit, Michigan.

As a child, Edison lost much of his hearing. It is unknown how it happened, but he viewed it as an advantage. Being partly deaf allowed him to think about his work without the distraction of noises around him.

In 1859 Edison quit school. He sold candy and newspapers on the railroad between Port Huron and Detroit, Michigan. He set up a chemistry laboratory on the train and tried out experiments! The railroad had recently begun using telegraph machines. The telegraph is a device for communicating over a distance. It uses electricity to send coded messages through wires. At the time, it was the fastest way to communicate over long distances. This was Edison's introduction to electrical machines.

When Edison was just 16, he traveled to different places working as a telegraph operator. At first, telegraph machines made dots and dashes on a strip of paper. They could be read and decoded. Newer telegraphs made sounds for the telegrapher to listen to. This made Edison's job

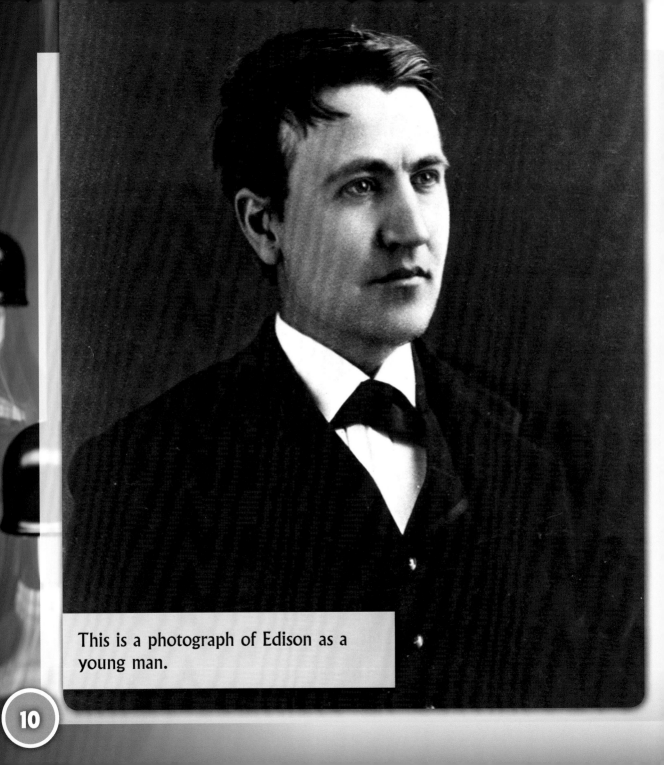

This is a photograph of Edison as a young man.

Quick Fact

During his career, Edison filed 389 patents for electric light and power, 195 for the phonograph, 150 for the telegraph, 141 for batteries, and 34 for the telephone!

harder because of his hearing loss. So he invented devices that made the job easier for him. Soon he stopped working as a telegraph operator so he could just work on his inventions.

In 1869, Edison got his first **PATENT**. It was for an electric vote-counting machine. The machine was not popular, but he learned from his failure. That same year Edison moved to New York City. His friend Franklin Pope let him sleep in a room at his office building.

Vocabulary Box

A **PATENT** is government approval to be the only person or company to make and sell a product.

When Edison fixed some machines there, he was hired to fix more! Soon after, Edison and Pope formed a business that made electrical machines.

During the next few years, Edison made several printing telegraphs. He was becoming known as a talented inventor. In 1874 he sold a telegraph that could send four messages at the same time. He also invented some of the earliest office equipment, including a printing machine called the mimeograph.

WRITE ONE
PRINT THE REST

Anything that you can typewrite can be duplicated exactly—a thousand times over—on the

EDISON OSCILLATING MIMEOGRAPH

So nearly automatic that it almost operates itself. An office boy can print 50 copies per minute. No errors, no omissions; each copy like the first. Ten times better than the original mimeograph. If you have to duplicate anything that you write, you need one. Write for our book.

A. B. Dick Company, 152-154 Lake Street, Chicago
Branch 47 Nassau Street, New York

Shown here is a 1901 advertisement for Edison's Oscillating Mimeograph. Mimeographs were widely used in businesses until the late 1960s, when many companies replaced them with photocopiers.

MENLO PARK

In 1876 Edison opened a laboratory in Menlo Park, New Jersey. He finally had a large workspace with all the tools he needed to do experiments. The following years were some of Edison's most creative. However, he did not do the work by himself.

In this photograph from 1904, Edison stands in his large laboratory in Menlo Park, New Jersey.

Edison hired talented people to help bring his ideas to life. These workers included a glassblower, a clock-maker, a mathematician, and other specialists. Edison also hired carpenters, machinists, draftsmen, book-keepers, secretaries, laboratory assistants, and a lawyer. These workers formed a successful team to help Edison accomplish his goals. They were able to research ideas and use what they learned to develop new products. This became a common way of working on new inventions and products in many areas.

Edison became known for working long hours, and he expected the same from his employees. They worked on several projects at the same time. Menlo Park soon became known as an invention factory.

Alexander Graham Bell invented the telephone in 1876, but it did not work that well. The sounds it made were hard to hear. It was an exciting invention, but it was not **PRACTICAL** for everyday use. Edison had an idea that made it better. His answer was a kind of microphone.

In this photograph, the inventor appears somewhat tired after five days and five nights of continuous work to make the perfect wax-cylinder type of phonograph.

This tiny device improved the quality of the sound in the telephone. For the first time, the telephone became a practical invention.

Edison's work with telegraphs and telephones led to the invention of

Vocabulary Box

An object is **PRACTICAL** if it can be used easily.

This is a drawing of Edison's first phonograph, which was created around 1877.

the phonograph, or record player. This invention used a needle and a cylinder coated with tinfoil to record and play back sounds. Edison amazed people across the country with his invention. However, interest wore off, and Edison turned his attention to other projects.

CHAPTER FOUR

IT'S ELECTRIC

In the 1800s the only way to light homes and businesses was with gas lamps. There were no lightbulbs. Several scientists began experimenting with using electricity to create light in the early 1800s. However, early lightbulbs were costly, unsafe, and did not last long. There was

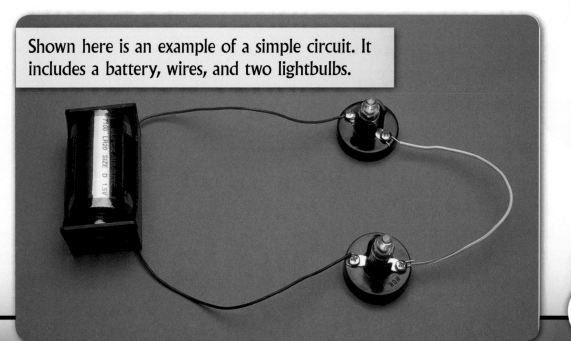

Shown here is an example of a simple circuit. It includes a battery, wires, and two lightbulbs.

also no good way to get the electricity to the lightbulbs. Most electrical systems used a process that connected all of the devices in a series circuit. That meant that if one lightbulb broke, the whole circuit broke, and then all the lights went out.

In 1878 Edison promised that he would produce a practical electric lightbulb to replace gas lighting. He also wanted to create an electrical system people could count on. He found several wealthy American businessmen to help set up the Edison Electric Light Company.

Even though he was a brilliant inventor, Edison did not have official training in science and math. So, he hired a scientist named Francis Upton. Upton's knowledge of math and physics helped Edison develop a practical lightbulb.

Other scientists had learned that a lightbulb could be made using a FILAMENT stretched between two wires. Edison knew that he

Vocabulary Box

A FILAMENT is a thin, threadlike wire. In a lightbulb it is heated by electricity until it glows brightly.

This illustration from an 1880 edition of *Scientific American* shows men manufacturing Edison's lightbulbs.

needed to create a lightbulb filament that could glow brightly without breaking. Edison experimented with many different filaments. He found a carbon material that worked well.

Edison also needed to create a stable electrical system to help keep a large area lit for longer than a

This photograph from 1880 shows Edison's Menlo Park laboratory shortly after it was wired for light.

Quick Fact

In 1882, the first lasting electrical power station was opened in New York City. It was designed and built by Edison.

few hours. He and Upton developed a parallel circuit. Instead of having all lightbulbs on the same path, a parallel circuit gives electricity different paths to travel through. If one lightbulb breaks, the rest keep glowing.

In December 1879 Edison kept his promise. He used electric lightbulbs to light his Menlo Park laboratory. For a few years he continued to improve his lightbulbs and electrical system. His work amazed people around the world.

BACK TO THE PHONOGRAPH, AND BEYOND

Other scientists were making their own electrical inventions. In the early 1880s, a Serbian scientist named Nikola Tesla came to the United States. He worked for Edison, but they argued about electricity and electrical systems. Edison was convinced direct current (DC) electricity was best. DC electricity can flow in only one direction. Tesla left Edison to develop **ALTERNATING** current (AC) electricity. AC electricity flows back and forth

Vocabulary Box

ALTERNATING means moving back and forth.

This portrait of Nikola Tesla was taken around 1890. Tesla was about 34 years old at the time.

quickly. Tesla sold his ideas to another inventor named George Westinghouse.

In 1893 Westinghouse was chosen over Edison to build a power plant in Niagara Falls, New York. The plant sent AC electricity 25 miles (40 km) away to Buffalo, New York. Tesla and Westinghouse had won the "War of Currents." AC electricity is what comes out of the outlets in your home. DC electricity is still used in batteries and solar cells.

In 1887 Edison opened a new laboratory in West Orange, New Jersey. As he continued to improve electrical lighting, he returned to the phonograph and made it better. The phonograph became a practical machine. Many people bought one. They also bought the products that went with it. Edison had created the recording industry.

In 1888 Edison began working on a camera that could record motion using film. He also created a machine called the Kinetoscope, which allowed people to view the

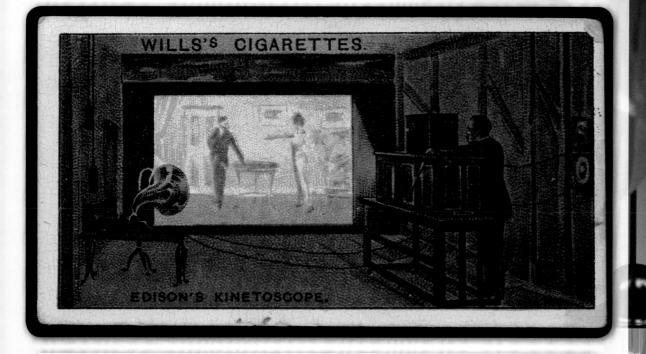

WILL'S CIGARETTES.

EDISON'S KINETOSCOPE.

This collectible card from 1915 shows one of Edison's early Kinetoscope theaters.

film. Edison showed his new machine to an audience in 1891. Soon he opened theaters in New York City. Edison produced machines for the public to buy, and he sold everything needed to use them, including movies! Edison had helped create the motion-picture business.

Edison stands next to a model for a concrete house around 1910.

In his later years Edison was less productive. However, he developed an electric battery for cars. He also had a very successful cement company. Edison cement was used to make buildings, roads, and dams. It was also used to build Yankee Stadium in the early 1920s!

Quick Fact

In 1910 Edison Studios in the Bronx, New York, created the first film featuring Frankenstein's monster. You can still see this movie today!

Edison was still hard at work up until his death in 1931. He had been working on a new way to make rubber for car tires. Without Edison's hard work, our world would be very different today.

TIMELINE

1847: Edison is born on February 11 in Milan, Ohio.

1854: Edison's father, Samuel, moves his family to Port Huron, Michigan, where he gets a job as a lighthouse keeper.

1859: Edison quits school and gets a job selling candy and magazines on the railroad between Port Huron and Detroit, Michigan.

1862: Edison saves a small boy from being hit by a train. The boy's father, another railroad employee, teaches Edison to use a telegraph.

1863: Edison becomes a full-time telegraph operator.

1869: Edison gets his first patent. It is for an electric vote-counting machine. The machine is not popular, but Edison learns a lot.

1869: Edison moves to New York City and gets a job fixing electrical machines for Samuel Laws' Gold Indicator Company.

1871: Edison sets up his first laboratory in Newark, New Jersey.

1874: Edison patents a telegraph machine that can send four messages at once.

1876: Edison opens his laboratory in Menlo Park, New Jersey.

1876: Alexander Graham Bell patents the first telephone.

1877: Edison develops the carbon transmitter, which makes the telephone a practical invention.

1877: Edison invents the phonograph.

1878: Edison founds the Edison Speaking Phonograph Company.

TIMELINE

1878: Edison begins working on electrical systems.

1879: Edison invents a lightbulb that lasts for more than 13 hours.

1882: Edison opens the first commercial electrical power plant for incandescent lighting in New York City.

1887: Edison opens a laboratory in West Orange, New Jersey, and perfects the phonograph.

1888: Edison begins work on a camera that can record motion. He will also invent a machine to show the film, called the Kinetoscope.

1891: Edison demonstrates his Kinetoscope for the public.

1894: The first Kinetoscope theater opens in New York City. This is the first public showing of motion pictures. The theater consisted of a row of Kinetoscopes. Each one could be used by only one person at a time.

1910: Edison Studios films and releases the first film showing Frankenstein's monster.

1911: Edison's many companies are grouped together and named Thomas A. Edison, Inc.

1929: Automobile industrialist Henry Ford holds a celebration honoring Edison on the 50th anniversary of Edison's lightbulb.

1931: Edison dies.

GLOSSARY

CARBON A common element used for many purposes.

DRAFTSMAN Someone who makes detailed technical plans and drawings.

ELECTRICITY A form of energy that is found in nature but that can be artificially produced.

EXPERIMENT A series of steps taken to discover something or to test an idea about something.

IMPRACTICAL Not easy to do or use.

INVENTOR Someone who makes new machines or products.

PHONOGRAPH A machine that can record and replay sounds.

PHYSICS A branch of science concerned with matter and energy and how they act.

PRACTICAL Suited for actual use.

SOLAR CELL A machine that turns sunlight into electricity.

TECHNOLOGY The use of knowledge to invent new devices or tools.

TELEGRAPH A machine used before the telephone to communicate over long distances. It used electricity to send messages in code.

FOR MORE INFORMATION

BOOKS

Brown, Don. *A Wizard from the Start: The Incredible Boyhood and Amazing Inventions of Thomas Edison.* Boston, MA: Houghton Mifflin Books for Children, 2010.

Garcia, Tracy J. *Thomas Edison.* New York, NY: PowerKids Press, 2013.

Kesselring, Susan. *Thomas Edison.* Mankato, MN: Child's World, 2010.

Rusch, Elizabeth. *Electrical Wizard: How Nikola Tesla Lit Up the World.* Somerville, MA: Candlewick Press, 2013.

Tourville, Amanda Doering. *Thomas Edison: Incredible Inventor.* Minneapolis, MN: Magic Wagon, 2013.

WEBSITES

Because of the changing nature of Internet links, Rosen Publishing has developed an online list of websites related to the subject of this book. This site is updated regularly. Please use this link to access the list:

http://www.rosenlinks.com/BBB/Edis

INDEX